THE

HORSE

SHOW

AT

MIDNIGHT

and

AN

AFTERNOON

OF

POCKET

BILLIARDS

THE
HORSE
SHOW
AT
MIDNIGHT *and*

AN
AFTERNOON
OF
POCKET
BILLIARDS

Poems by
HENRY TAYLOR

LOUISIANA STATE UNIVERSITY PRESS   Baton Rouge and London
1992

Copyright © 1966, 1975, 1992 by Henry Taylor
All rights reserved
Manufactured in the United States of America
First printing

01 00 99 98 97 96 95 94 93 ·92   5 4 3 2 1
The Horse Show at Midnight was first published by Louisiana State University Press in 1966. *An Afternoon of Pocket Billiards* was first published by the University of Utah Press in 1975.

Designer: G. Phoebe
Typeface: Sabon
Typesetter: Graphic Composition, Inc.
Printer and binder: Thomson-Shore, Inc.

Grateful acknowledgment is made to the publishers of the following journals and anthologies, in which poems in *The Horse Show at Midnight* first appeared: *The Beloit Poetry Journal, Cargoes, The Chronicle of the Horse, The Georgia Review, The New Mexico Quarterly, New Writing from Virginia* (New Writing Associates, 1963), *Plume & Sword, Shenandoah, The Sixties, Stylus,* and *The University of Virginia Magazine.* Thanks are also due to the publishers of the following journals and anthologies, in which poems in *An Afternoon of Pocket Billiards* first appeared: *The American Oxonian, Appalachian Journal, Book Week, Café Solo, Calliope's Comments, Cargoes, Carolina Quarterly, Cimarron Review, Contempora, The Daily Utah Chronicle, Encounter, Epos, Folio, Friends Journal, The Hollins Alumnae Magazine, The Hollins Critic, Messages* (Little, Brown & Company, 1973), *The Michigan Quarterly Review, Mill Mountain Review, Monmouth Review, New Mexico Quarterly, New Writing from Virginia, The New York Quarterly, Noise Quarterly, Poems from Italy* (Thomas Y. Crowell Co., 1972), *Poetry Northwest, Poetry: Points of Departure* (Winthrop Publishers, 1974), *Practical Horseman, Pucred, Roanoke Review, Shenandoah, Southern Poetry Review, The Southern Review, Southern Writing in the Sixties: Poetry* (Louisiana State University Press, 1967), *Tennessee Poetry Journal, The Transatlantic Review, The Virginia Quarterly Review, Wasatch Front,* and *The Western Humanities Review.*
     "Bernard and Sarah," "Breakings," "Buildings and Grounds," "Burning a Horse," "Campaign Promise," "Riding Lesson," and "Speech" were published in 1971 in *Breakings,* a limited edition produced by The Solo Press, San Luis Obispo, California.
     Lines from "No Man's Good Bull" from *Let Not Your Hart,* copyright © 1970 by James Seay. Reprinted by permission of the author and University Press of New England. Lines from "Ecloga III" from *The Eclogues and the Georgics of Virgil,* copyright © 1971, 1972 by David R. Slavitt. Reprinted by permission of the author and Johns Hopkins University Press. Lines from *Riding and Jumping,* copyright © 1969 by William Steinkraus. Reprinted by permission of the author and Doubleday & Company. English translation of the poetry of Giuseppe Ungaretti published with the permission of Cornell University Press.

Library of Congress Cataloging-in-Publication Data

Taylor, Henry, 1942—
    [Horse show at midnight]
    The horse show at midnight ; and, An afternoon of pocket billiards
    : poems / by Henry Taylor.
        p.   cm.
    ISBN 0-8071-1777-3 (alk. paper).—ISBN 0-8071-1763-3 (pbk. :
alk. paper)
    I. Taylor, Henry, 1942— Afternoon of pocket billiards. 1992.
II. Title. III. Title: Horse show at midnight. IV. Title:
Afternoon of pocket billiards.
PS3570.A93A6   1992
811'.54—dc20   91-41119
                                                                          CIP

The paper in this book meets the guidelines for permanence and durability of the Committee on Production Guidelines for Book Longevity of the Council on Library Resources. ∞

CONTENTS

AUTHOR'S NOTE

This is a complete reissue of *The Horse Show at Midnight* (1966) and *An Afternoon of Pocket Billiards* (1975), so I have not dropped any poems; however I think they represent me now, they are a fair representation of who and where I was when they were first collected. There are just a dozen instances of a word or phrase altered or a line deleted; they are all changes I made during the first year of each book's existence, when public readings and private reactions helped me hear what I had done or meant to do. Many adjustments have occurred to me since, but they sound like the meddling of someone other than the author of the poems, whom I recall with diminishing clarity.

The Horse Show at Midnight was for Sarah; the acknowledgments included thanks for help and guidance from Fred Bornhauser, Richard Dillard, Eleanor Fletcher and the Noonday Bookshop, Walter Fletcher, George Garrett, Louis Rubin, May Sarton, and William Jay Smith. *An Afternoon of Pocket Billiards* was for George Garrett, Louis Rubin, William Jay Smith, and Tom Taylor, old artificers. My wife Frannie has been an inspiring and sustaining presence throughout the adventures of most of these poems.

My association with Louisiana State University Press has been long and friendly; it is a profound pleasure to have virtually all of my poems under their imprint. L. E. Phillabaum, Margaret Dalrymple, Catherine Landry, and Michael Pinkston have earned more of my gratitude than I can express. And as long as I remember anything, I will remember the patient care with which Miller Williams, Charles East, Robert L. Nance, and Mary Alice Hemstreet treated the first printing of my first book.

. . . and yet if you ride confidently and well,
and ask confidently and soundly for the
horse's best level of performance, his
response will be to the ride you give him,
and not to your secret thoughts.
—*William Steinkraus,* Riding and Jumping

THE

HORSE

SHOW

AT

MIDNIGHT

I

In Medias Res

I had a Latin master once
Whose name was J. B. Laramore.
One year we read of arms and men
And memorized the motto of
The University of Chicago:

Let knowledge grow from more to more
And so be human life enriched.
He also taught what he called *tact*—
Satiric, exaggerated respect
("Now when you get to be my age—"

"Almost old enough to vote, sir!")
For those whose age was so near ours
They might have been insulted by
Honest pretense at subservience.
He sat before us in the afternoon

And drummed into our memories
Vergil's verses, in small doses:
Perhaps someday thoughts of these things
Will bring us joy. "The tears at the heart
Of things . . ." interminable pause—

"omnia migrant: all things change."
The last day I saw him, he called
An early halt to the final exam,
And asked us all to leave.
Silently we filed beside his desk

While he gazed, speechless, at the window.
I did not see him at graduation.
I like to think he was afraid to come.
When I had my diploma in my hand,
I locked the door of a cinderblock room
And left love and my Latin book behind.

Three Snapshots

for George Garrett

1 *A Death in the Family*

Ed Harrington came to the door
One time, and spoke to my father.
"You ain't got any old dark suit
You want to expose of, is you?
My wife's brother's wife
Has gone and joined the air crew."

"How did she die?" my father asked.
"Deed I don't know, Mister Tom.
She went down into the cellar
To get some fruit or somethin',
And just ceased down there."

2 *Blackberries*

On top of a ragged hill on the farm
Next to my father's, an old man
Sat on his front porch and reigned
Over a dominion of thistles and briars.

In his meadow, never mowed,
Blackberries grew wild, overran
The field, smothered the grass,
Bound the cows and ate them alive.

My sisters and I would steal
Under his fence, armed with pails,
To pick as many berries as we could.
We never got them all, hard as we tried.

One afternoon we stood in the briars
Reaching for berries over our heads,
Each one hanging before us like a bunch
Of grapes, when down from his porch

The old man tumbled, down the hill
Toward us, wild white hair in the wind,
Scattering all of his chickens as he ran.
His tiny dog yapped at his heels.

"Go back where you belong right now!"
And he waved his arms. We turned
And ran for the fence, clutching the pails
In our arms, scattering berries behind us.

We looked back once and saw him on the hill,
Shaking his fist in the wind and shouting.
"If you're too lazy to raise your own
Blackberries, by God, you shan't have mine!"

3   *Mule Trader*

Not long after the mule we'd had
For years had died, my father
Saw the man we'd bought it from.
He had a face so brown and hard
It would crack to pieces if he smiled.

"How's the finest mule I ever sold?"
My father told him the mule was dead.
"You, sir, are a God damn liar!
I been selling mules for forty years,
And I ain't *never* heard of one dying!"

The Stones of Emptiness

When Cortez came to Mexico,
Crawled, rushed, clambered, swept
Into the city of the Aztecs, he found
A tribe of handsome holy men
As ancient as the gods, who
Nursed, indulged, and fed
For a year their human sacrifices
To the hungry and inexorable
Tenants of their temple, then led
Them joyfully up the steps of stone
To the pinnacle of the pyramid.
There, in one small consecrated room,
Upon an altar like a slab, those boys
Lay down and let their hearts
Be taken as they lived and breathed.
Blood ran, fell, spurted from their
Wounds, and stained the walls
Until, after centuries had passed,
Huge scabs hung even from the ceiling.
Flutes as well as priests escorted
Those young and satiated boys
Up the heavy steps, and were broken
Before the temple's open doors.
But Cortez and his stainless soldiers
Stood in that Aztec city,
Above those brown and quiet men,
And commanded, with their long unwielded swords,
That these inhuman heathen rites must cease.

They feared to tear the temple down.

Now, among the crumbling Aztec temples
Wide women walk, with husbands
Bearing cameras and straw hats,
Their feet an ignorant and continual
Irreverent shuffle on the tile.
They look about from time to time, and nod,
And ask their guides how old the temple is.
The walls reverberate, and their questions
Echo back. The answer is the music
Of those shattered flutes, that hangs
Still on the musty air, a prayer
For those vanished civilized and holy men.

No blood runs down those cold stones now.

Over the River and Through the Woods

High in a house above a city
My grandmother has waited
For the last thirty years
With the sight going out of her eyes.

At last, it is whispered
By sisters and aunts
In tones of relieved condescension
That my mother's mother is dying
Because of a cancer in her blood.

My parents, who have never been
Her eyes, bestow on me the guilt
Of their neglect, and force me
To feel compelled to visit her.

Reluctantly, experimentally,
I walk into the room
Which she has darkly decorated
For the likes of me.

Fearful of bacteria, she
Will not let me take her hand,
But clasps her own two hands
In a gesture of greeting
And shakes them in the air.

For a little more than an hour
She tells me all the important things.
Daily, in front of a window,
She marches in place for exercise.

She has an ingrown toenail
Which her doctor forbids her to cut.
My sisters keep secrets from her,
She says, and the walls eavesdrop
On our conversation.

Gratefully, patiently she sits
As I take my leave,
Clasping her shaking hands,
Saying goodbye to the chair
I have been sitting in.

I am lowered down through the house
And I walk through the door
Out onto the street,
Back to my own more familiar
Decaying picture of things.

Remembering Kevan MacKenzie

Once upon a time I spent a summer
At a camp for children far from here,
Teaching riding to young boys and girls.
I taught them to make a horse go straight,
The way to make a horse stand still.
They grew and danced like weeds before my eyes.

Now there remains in my mind's eye
One face of all the faces of that summer;
It smiles at me, and I sit here
Wondering what's become of all the girls
That Kevan MacKenzie hounded straight
To earth, and may be chasing still.

Every week there was a dance, and still
I can recall the roll of those girls' eyes
As they hunted love, the first of summer:
Kevan, refusing to dance, stood straight
By the wall and dared the girls
To rout him from his sanctuary here.

Later he began to dress with care, and here
I remember the guarded gleam in his eye
As he came through the door and went straight
For the oldest and prettiest girl,
While with that stare that disturbs me still
The young girls hunted the first love of summer.

In the arms of that tall breath of summer
He danced, and looked her waist in the eye.
I whispered then, "Be cheerful, girls,

The sunshine boys are here."
When the music at last grew still,
The tall girl smiled, once more stood straight.

The days of dancing and love rode straight
To the last long week of that summer.
When I said goodbye to my boys and girls
I stood among them with tears in my eyes,
While Kevan MacKenzie, smiling still,
Said, "You must be glad to get out of here."

Now I sit here in another summer
And rising straight in my mind's eye
Kevan and his girls are dancing still.

For Mary Jay, Practicing Archery

Barefoot, armed to the teeth
With a forty-pound bow, dressed
In a two-piece bathing suit,
My sister marches forth against
Six numbered colored plastic circles.

Oh, she knows what the boys
Will say about this exercise,
How brazenly it gleams with hope
For the shape of things to come.
But as she stands before that

Target filled with straw, she sees
Those numbers on the hearts of men,
Dreams of soft-eyed deer and flying birds.
She takes good aim for the highest score.
She dreams her feet as fleet as Atalanta's

And wishes for the runner who will
Summon up the speed to master her.
The sun shines on her careful hair.
When they are gone, she goes and pulls
The arrows out with care between

Her fingers, then returns to the foul line,
Placing the arrows one by one
Into the quiver fringed with suede,
And the ancient huntress runs once more
Among those hard grey hills.

A Bargain at Half the Price

for Steve Canty

On a blasted heath in Maryland
There stands a livestock auction house
Where, every other Wednesday, men come
From miles around to buy and sell
Cheap saddles, swap lies and horses.
One night, I remember, they
Auctioned off one hundred plastic
Crucifixes, one at a time.

Riders in cowboy boots and red
T-shirts take the horses
Up the aisle and back, while
The auctioneer, known as Honest John,
Pries loose the bids and shouts them out.
"Sixty dollars! God damn it,
Gentlemen, let us pray!"
In the stands men drink big
Orange drinks and sit with girls
In tight blue slacks, with dyed black hair.

Once a month, from somewhere comes
A little man with a big trunk.
He stands in the center of the ring
And pulls out halters, buckets,
Reins, a saddle with one stirrup
("Here, gentlemen, we have a saddle
For a one-legged man!"), until
You think he has some magic power.

Someone has said that once a man
Walks through the doors of X's

Livestock Market, he is forever
Doomed. He may be right. I like
To think that while he stands
Beneath that roof, it is sanctuary,
And for anything he says or does
God has forgiven him already.

A Story for My Mother

One begins at an early age to know
The standard relationships—that fathers
Always have wives who have to be mothers.
The young think pairs, not broken halves; so
When my mother's thin, blind father began
To become known to us, we children had
To ask where his wife was, and hear she was dead.
We could never ask where she was again.
We learned to love the ones who had to hold
His elbow when he walked, who lived with him
And tried to help him push a way through life.
We played at Blind Man's Bluff till we were old
Enough to blush, wonder, and pity him
His dark and windy days without a wife.

Two things were told when my grandfather died.
I learned his wife was still alive, and why
No one had told us. Driving through the night, my
Father said she'd lost her mind, and I tried
To understand the ways some people hide.
So the time had come to tell us now, I
Knew, because the news would break, my eye
Would move across the fine newsprint: "Survived
By his wife. . . ." I think of those words often.
She'd sat there, acknowledging no one's presence,
Weekly ignoring my grandfather. I find
I forget what I knew of his existence,
Think only of his lips sewn shut in the coffin,
And the way her presence has crowded my mind.

Three hours of an evening nap were gone
When the phone brought me lurching from my bed
To hear my father's quiet voice push down
Through miles and hours of sleep into my head
To let me know my grandmother had died
And that there would be services next day
If I could come. If not, he understood: he'd tried
To reach me earlier. I could not come away,
And turned to sleep and dreams of work not done,
And did not think of that phone call for what seemed
Like hours. Later, stung by snow-reflected sun,
I wondered if the call were real or dreamed.
If I fear to ask about her any more,
Mother, understand me: things are as they were.

The Female Graduate Student

Almost constantly, I find myself
Stumbling on a stairway
Or sugaring the saucer

Where I was quite sure the cup
Should have been. Oh, yes,
I still present papers

Of a highly professional nature,
Superficially. But no one
Really believes me:

I cannot get poetry published.
I would get out
Of this place,

Except, of course, for the lease,
And the things I have purchased
On time.

The Circus Rider's Departure

for May Sarton

I

For years, in one of three red rings,
Above my horse, with arms like wings,

Balanced on one leg or arm,
I have traced circles in sawdust,

Swung down to soft sawdust to turn
Handsprings beside my horse's hooves.

The silent crowds that gaze to learn
What spins my sequined, silver clothes

Have not seen through to hours that must
Be spent imagining true form—

In empty tents, in muffled rings,
Rehearsing nonexistent things,

Tricks to seem to know what no one knows.

II

I worked for years: at first, merely
Astride, my feet in the stirrups,

Then standing up, then each handspring
In turn, each trick built on the things

Mastered before. There always come
The next things to be mastered, some

Somersault or balanced attitude,
Some sleight of hand or foot or horse

Which has not been attempted yet.
The time comes when there is no more

To learn, except what is too hard,
Impossible except in thought, and so

There are no further tricks to learn.
The essence of deception now

Is making practiced, easy tricks
Difficult and not difficult,

So that those gazers wonder how
The thing is done, and wonder why

The same thing is too hard for them.
The trick itself comes thoughtlessly.

The trick becomes an act of mind:
Reveal some evidence of strain,
Conceal that which cannot be learned.

III

So this was where I stood tonight.
The mirror in my dressing room

Reflected clothes in perfect order,
And yet some nameless thing was missing.

I could not see what was not right,
And so I rode into the ring,

Standing on my cantering horse,
My arms outstretched, my practiced smile

Arrested in its proper place.
As my body and my horse revolved

Among the wickets I had placed,
The trick that could not be performed

Became itself inside my mind:
The faces in the chairs came clear,

Reflecting the light on my face.
Not now. I turned one last handspring,

Dismounted, bowed, and left the ring.
The feel of sawdust on my hand

Is pleasant, but I know it now.
The trick I do not dare perform

Unfolds along my waiting frame
And I can see through it, beyond

Performing it, to further hours
Of work, a cycle without end:

Another trick begins to show its face.

IV

And now the crowds have all gone home,
Lighting the dark with their faces.

Out in the evening now, I see
The clowns moving through deepening dark

In overalls, with trunks and pails.
My horse breathes softly beside me.

Slow as steamshovels, elephants
Exhale their last tubs of water.

The spectators all have departed,
The tigers are back in their cages.

The great brown octopus shadow
Of tent is down and folded now.

A whistle blows. I stand and watch
The painted train move down the rails.

Darkness descends on this suburb;
I have ridden my last matinee.

Beneath no lights I take the reins,
And I place my foot in a stirrup.
Slowly, astride, I ride away.

II

Mr. James Dickey in Orbit

The darkness is closing around us
And the loudspeaker calls out the hours
In seconds of waiting.
High in my tower of steel and fuel
Which points to the stars,

Bravely phallic,
I lie strapped to my seat
In a spacesuit.

The instruments cluster around me.
I give each of them one final handshake.
I close my eyes when the time comes,
Nestling down in my long chair.
As the weight of my body presses

Down into me, the colors
Pass in front of my eyes,
The glorious purple of Heaven.
The thunder of engines enraged
Makes the tower quiver in terror.

I rise, I float from the ground,
Into the heavenly purple.
For the moment, there is nothing
But darkness.
But the rocket knows what it is doing.
And it bends its course in a circle.
I look through the electrical eyes
And I see my green earth below me.
I shout three green cheers for myself.

The black sky resounds with my joy.
The stars, incredibly bright,
Shine through the blackness toward me.
In the blue of my joy I salute them.
Re-entry into the earth's air
Begins after my third tour of the sky.

I start my brave plunge to the ocean,
Exulting in the thunder of sun,
Of engines no longer enraged,
But burnt out.
My happy comrades are waving

From the deck of the ship that awaits me.
I shout as I crash into the sea.
I feel the capsule slow down,
And bob back up to the surface.
Blackness closes around me.

I hear the voice of my captain
Come over the loudspeaker toward me.
The blastoff has been postponed again.
There is weather over the ocean.

I greet the sad face of my captain,
And I smile.
His perplexity does not disturb me.
I climb down from my tower in triumph:
Tonight I have marched through the heavens.
I shout three green cheers for myself.

J. V. Cunningham Gets Hung Up
on a Dirty, of All Things, Joke

Love, I have lain awake by night
And tried to get the punch line right,

And tried to keep, with fierce intent,
A firm grasp of my instrument;

Though words are scarce and thought is thick
My flawless grammar is the trick

By which, though I am short of wit
And slow to make my couplets fit,

I shall explain, with love and luck,
Three Chinese sailors and a duck.

Howard Nemerov Experiences
Another Statue

Approximately a month ago—
Perhaps it was last week—no,
I believe it was yesterday.
I don't quite remember, really.
Anyway, as I walked in the park,
A funny thing happened to me.

Stout, of course, and upon
A pedestal, naturally enough,
Stood a statue of someone.
There were people all over
The place, newsboys, lovers,
And a man selling nuts.

Nobody else seemed to notice
What the statue did then.
As I gazed on it, it became
Transfigured before my eyes,
And it did a thing that seemed
To me remarkable, perhaps obscene.

As I said, no one took any notice.
I am sorry about that, in a way,
Because now you may not wish
To believe me. But it did that,
Honest it did, and so I thought
I would tell you about it.

A Conversation Between a Man and a Woman Who Talk as if They Were, Respectively, Robert Creeley and Denise Levertov

HE: Woman came
        myself to woo
and with her came
        my coming too.

SHE: Why must you always either
make your mazing overtures
or relate in undertones
        adventures in a tense
so past? Which do you do?

HE: Fine,
        thank you
very much.
        And you?

SHE: Not so hot
                as it was
even in monotonic shadows
           of mud huts
in Mexico where not a thing was new
               is love like this.

HE: In fact
        we move
in act
        of love—

SHE: An act not simple,
                       not baroque,
      remarkable in its
                eloquence,
      eloquent in its
                remarkableness.

HE: Somehow, sweetheart,
      I suspect
    that you have changed
      the subject.

SHE: Here in this room of purple shadows,
    my bearded, hairy-handed friend,
    the little worlds of our red eyes revolve
    so certainly that neither you nor I
    can ever say for sure.

George Garrett Gets at the Root
of the Matter

Once, walking in the woods,
I came to a clump of Jack-in-
the-Pulpits, dancing in the breeze,
shaken by the Spirit, shouting from
under their canopies Are You Saved.
I pulled one up. The root a bulb.

I cut a little piece of it with
my knife and tasted it. Lay
on my tongue like raw potato,
then, after a time, took fire, burned
my tongue as pepperoni never did
in Rome, or artillery fire in Trieste.

Let someone else decide why
such a root held down that
holy figure. All I know is,
I walked for miles before
I found a spring, and cold
clear water tasted good.

James Wright Is Depressed by the Death of the Horse That He Bought from Robert Bly

Never have I seen the sky more clear
Than in Montana. Birds with eyes
Inside my bones confuse this clarity.
I stand here in this Montana field
Remembering when things were as they were,
And watch the silent eyes of a horse
Which I recently bought from a friend.

Small creatures are talking among themselves
In the grass around my shoes.
I discover, to my surprise
(For lack of a better word),
That the horse did not belong to my friend
In the first place.

Alone, alone, I sink to my knees
In the grass by an ownerless horse
And weep for all students of Spanish.
Minnesota is what I meant to say,
And they may never know.

And Robert Bly Says Something, Too

I

I wake to find myself lying in an open field.
About my head the ends of grasses
Wave softly in the wind.

II

I raise my head and turn on my side
And see a horse's tail swishing at flies.
It is attached to the end of a horse.

III

In my way I love to consider things I love—
Oh, often even in summer in this kind of field
I think I should be covered up with snow!

III

Things Not Solved Though Tomorrow Came

For whether lighted over ways that save
Or lured from all repose,
If he go on too far to find a grave,
Mostly alone he goes.
        —E. A. Robinson

There is silence in this blue car now.
My daughter and I have driven for hours
Through early morning, where we started,
High noon on the turnpike, where we stopped
To eat in a pink brick restaurant,
On through to afternoon, the hour when
The sun shines on the sides of golden things,
Until we are struck dumb by nearness to the end,
The long green shadows of her boarding school
Where we are bound, where we arrive at last.

We unload the car in several trips,
Carrying up the stairs to the third floor
Her clothes, her blankets, pennants, lamps,
Stuffed animals. The job at last is done.
She stands before me, smiling, as I lean
Against the car, my hand on my thick waist,
Trying not to sweat or gasp for breath.
It is time for me to leave. She kisses me
On the forehead.
                "Goodbye, sweetheart," I say.
"We'll miss you. Hit the books. Write home some time."

She kisses me once more, then walks away.
I think of last year at this time,
Her first year here, when neither she
Nor I could keep tears back for long.
She walks across the dying, dark green grass,
Her brown hair, her mother's hair, shining
As it comes between my eyes and the sun.
Some friends of hers are waiting on the porch—

A tall boy smiles, and she begins
To line up love in the nick of time.

Autumn is descending on this hemisphere;
Leaves are turning now, in Pennsylvania.
The sun is shining on the sides of things,
And another summer has come to an end.
I climb into my car and turn for home—
I have far to go, and not much time.
My daughter's face is formed inside my mind
And I say to it,
                    "When you were born,
Light of my life, I could not in
My wildest dreams imagine you like this."

———

I am alone in my blue car once more.
You are home safe, and I turn south
Trying to retain some sense of your presence
At my side, some sound, but all I hear
Is silence deeper than our speechlessness.
My mind turns slowly back through these
Brown leaves, to autumns of my childhood.

In the cellar, in a spacious crate,
I kept a lamb until it died.
My father gave me another, and I tried
To feed it clover blooms and bottled milk.
I fed it every morning, every night.
One winter Saturday I slept late;
When I awoke, the sun was high, shone
Through dead leaves of trees outside my window.
I rose and heated the bottle of milk,
Went down the stairs and stood on my toes
To lean over the side of the crate.
The lamb lay still, would not arise.
I stood there for what may have been an hour,
Staring down at those dull and dusty eyes,
And thought of rabbits I had kept out back
The year before, and how the babies bled

To death one night when a weasel
Got through a hole I had not patched that day.

Darkness comes upon me on the road.
Before I assail the windy turnpike
I have to stop for coffee, noise and light.
There is a diner up ahead, next to a motel
Which advertises Rest For Weary Bones.
Inside, the clock above the smoking grill
Says eight-fifteen. I take a booth beside
The window, and watch the highway wind away.
A young girl brings a menu and a glass
Of water and stands above me, pencil poised,
Moving in time to the jukebox music
Which I had not heard until I looked at her.

I order only coffee. As she turns
Away she winks and asks me if I'm tired.
Daughter, your feet upon the dying grass
Did not move as hers do, dancing on these tiles.

When she returns she slides into the booth
Across from me, searches for three jukebox tunes
To spend my quarter on, and, as she touches
My hand and smiles, I see through coffee steam
And smoke the eyes that looked through me at lunch
This afternoon;
                they tell me I have far
To go, but I have stopped for now.
                                    She lifts
The little jar of cream which I had left
Untouched beside the sugar bowl, holds it
Before her face as if to offer me
A toast, then drinks it down in one small gulp.

She smiles, and we sit talking now about
Where I have been, where I am going, how
She likes her work and why she does it.
The things I say are of no consequence,
Regardless of the effort I have made.

I forget words as I speak them, only note
Her nod, her eyes, how hard it is for me
To keep my daughter's voice from drowning hers,
To keep the world beyond the foggy window
From moving through the dark outside until
The lines that hold me to it are cast off
At last, and I am left with nothing but
Her face, the things our fingers touch, words I forget . . .

Daughter, I speak to her of you, say you
Are beautiful, think to myself that you
Must never know how, when I speak,
Hers becomes the face whose eyes I praise.

Hours, cigarettes, and cups of coffee
Find us sitting at this table still,
Her fingers touching mine.
                      The man behind
The counter tells us it is time to leave.
I notice, as he speaks to her, a tone
Not at all familiar, as if we both
Were customers. I rise and start to say
It's Been Nice Talking To You, but no words
Come. She finds her coat and brings it to me;
I help her into it as if I had
Done so a thousand times before,
And we depart, when I have paid the man
Behind the counter, arm in arm.

We stand still outside for a moment,
Until we can see each other in this dark.
I suppose she must be twenty-five or so.
Daughter, love, I say to you I see in her
Eyes a thing I have not seen in yours,
A thing no one I've loved has let me see
For years. We do not speak.
                      She gets into
My car while I walk across the road
To the office of the motel, speak to
Someone, pay him money, go out with the key.

Speechless in the car, we cross the road
Together, get out and stand beside the door,
My hand on her elbow.
                          It is cold out here,
Perhaps for the first time, I tell myself,
This fall. At home, where lights have probably
Gone out, late treefrogs may be speaking still
By the pond at the end of the driveway.
You have unpacked your things and gone to bed,
Thinking perhaps of the tall boy who smiled
At you this afternoon,
                          and I stand here
With this strange waitress, thinking thoughts I have
Not thought for years and years—
                                    How one must act
At times like this to keep the moment real,
Create a world out of thin air: to keep
Things going as they are supposed to go.

———

Inside, attempts at speech in the dim light
Of the desk lamp, then silence as before.
She comes into my arms for a minute
Or two, then disengages me and sits
Along the bed's edge, lights two cigarettes,
And holds one out to me ambiguously:
Daring or inviting me to sit down.
I sit down close to her and take her hand;
We smoke in silence for a time.
                                    Why did
You bring me here? I almost ask, but know
That her reply would sound the same.
                                       She rises,
Then crosses to the desk, close to the light,
And starts to take her clothes off. I undo
My tie, then stop and look at her. Her white
Waitress's uniform, unbuttoned at
The front, slides slowly down over shoulders
And hangs about her hips.

                              I have come far
To find this room, this creaking bed, this light
That plays such tricks upon my eyes and on
Her hands and hair;
                              I think at this moment
I shall be here forever while all things
Grow old around me, pass me in the dark,
And I shall lie tortured in this cavern
Until death, or madness, comes.
                              But now,
Straight from a pile of clothes upon her feet
She rises, moves into my arms,
An island rising from the sea.

———————

Now I lie here on this dishevelled bed
Relaxing my tense muscles one by one.
Remembering an old consideration
Born of an old embarrassment, I try
To drift toward sleep without moving a hand
Or breathing too loudly. I fall closer
To sleep, but feel something stir in my brain
And recognize a shame from years ago,
Remembering how, at school, I stained my
Underwear behind locked doors, night after night.
Longer ago than that, I crouched at night
In bed on all fours, sitting on my feet,
And rocked back and forth singing to myself
Or dreaming of the time I would be free,
And fell, at last, forward on my face,
Put my thumb into my mouth, and fell asleep.

And at this moment, as I fall toward sleep
I sense in this tenseness in
My arm the effort to keep
My hand, my thumb, beside me.

———————

I dream of rabbits the weasel killed,
Of lambs that died in my care.

When I wake, I am sitting up in bed.
This girl is gone, whose eyes shone with some thing
I had not seen for years till now, whose voice
Moved in me even through dark clouds of sleep.
I try to bring her face before my eyes,
But all I can remember is the way
Her dress hung on her hips as she stood before me.
It is still dark outside, and still.
In the hundred miles ahead of dark
Turnpike I will have time enough to try
To remember faces, in that roaring chill.

I lie down and light a fresh cigarette.
I roll over on my stomach and stretch,
Then drop the cigarette in one instant
Of the coldest dread, one moment so short
It could contain but one impression, to be thought
About forever after it.
                              In that
Instant, a giant thing stood over me:
Its legs were at my shoulders, hips and feet,
Its heavy, shining wings clapped on its back;
I do solemnly swear I heard its breath,
And felt its rasping jaws above my neck.
Oh, daughter, darling, what can this thing be?
Can it have been so wrong that you loved me?

I rise from bed and take the road once more. The car
Rolls through the darkness
      as a fierce beast runs through cold,
Extinguishing a whispered calling in my ear.
Of what is past, I only know what I am told—
I can no longer tell whose voice is in the air.
Headlights try for secrets the road will always hold:
There are things I have not seen
      though I have been to where they are.

One Summer Night

I lie and listen to thunder and rain
And gaze at lightning reflected
On the wet leaves of trees outside
Until, through the darkness, I hear
The voice of my son, and I rise
And go down the hall to his room.

The storm shines in through the window
And I see that his bed is empty.
I run down to the lawn and call
To my slender, pale-haired son,
And his voice comes down from above me.
He is standing on top of the house,

His arms held away from his sides,
Looking down at me and smiling.
I ask him to come down.
On the peak of the roof he turns
And raises his eyes to the sky.
Rain falls from his hair to his back.

Once more lightning flashes
As he flexes his knees and leaps
Upward, his arms close at his sides.
He tilts his head and raises his arms
And begins his back-dive to earth,
Eyes closed and hair windblown.

He slows down in front of my face,
Upside down before my eyes,
His arms overhead toward earth.

I ask him again to come down.
We are caught there together, immobile
In a flash of lightning which lasts forever

And I call to him time after time
But he is unable to answer.
Smiling, his blue eyes closed,
His arms overhead toward earth,
His blond hair waving like seaweed,
He hangs helpless and silent before me.

A Blind Man Locking His House

The tall clock in the hallway strikes
The half-hour chime:
Twelve-thirty. Now the hour has come
For footsteps in the dark, that like
To wander through this house from room to room.

My wife and I live here alone,
So my wife thinks;
But in the dark my dark eye blinks,
Down passageways of pure unknown
The hunter starts to stalk, and my heart sinks.

I rise and gird myself to face
This sounding house,
One hand stretched out against the blows
From chairs that will not stay in place,
From anarchy that sightlessness allows,

The other rummaging for keys
In my coat pocket.
At each door, as I pause to lock it,
Relentless blood assails my eyes
And drives them crazy: useless in their sockets,

They still roll upward in my head.
By force of will
I aim them downward: through this chill,
Pretending to look straight ahead,
I make the footsteps think I see, until

Between me and this heavy tread
At least one door
Is safely locked. From door to door
I pass, and learn I am misled:
There is no safe place for me any more.

To such thoughts does this presence tempt me
As floorboards creak
That I might drive myself to break
My heart at last, and find it empty,
Because some thing stalks me and will not speak.

The hallway clock clangs like my heart,
In time with feet
That flee, and press behind, and meet
At last, and all of this is part
Of all this house. My pitiful conceit

Breaks down, and I shall not escape.
Older than air
Or the stairway, he is somewhere
In dust and stone that saps all hope;
When I lie down that sound will still be there.

Time and again my wife has said
No one is there;
But in the weather of despair
As I climb up through dark to bed
I hear his step behind me on the stair.

A Dream of a Distant Land

Deep in a darkness many weeks old
I stand alone at the rail of my ship
Listening to the sounds to which
I have not yet become accustomed:
The pump of engines nudging the boat
Through the clear, cold, endless night;
The crack of icebergs that surround,
But do not bind me; and forever
The crash of water on a coast
Where seals on the rocks move slowly.
On the deck, now, I am alone,
Only thinking of you, waiting
Where thoughts of ice and whales
Are rarely more than amusements,
But I know that below me men watch
The hands of curious instruments tremble,
Hunting for the best course south
To the Arctic Circle, the open sea,
Back home to the Temperate Zones,
Where I played as a boy in the first
Cold winds of autumn among shocks
Of corn covered with frost, and walked
In the fields where my father's cattle
Lived. Through the open window
At night I could hear horses
Cantering across a field of stubble,
Steering around the shocks of corn
One night when they got out
Like polar bears cruising among
The icebergs as they swim beside
My ship in the clothing of life

Itself: claws, eyes, teeth and hair,
Salt water running in their veins
As it runs in yours and mine.
I think of you waiting for me
In this land where summer is short
Enough to force you to remember winter.
Through the veins of the bear,
In your brain and in mine,
The blood that knows will blunder
Its way from season into season,
As it sends the fish beneath me
Through the dark, like horses
Dodging frozen white shocks of corn
On a stubble sea, their senses
Of direction trembling like the hands
On the dials of careful instruments below
That guide me to you from breaking waves
Where seals on the rocks move slowly.

The Horse Show at Midnight

I *The Rider*

Now, the showground is quiet.
The spectators all have departed.
Along the walls of the arena
The jumps are lying, collapsed.
The moon shines down on the grandstand
As I walk out across the ring
Alone, watching for what may not be here.
I take my place as a judge
In the center of the ring, waiting.
Asleep in their stables, the horses
Awaken to my thought-out call
And rise from the straw and walk
To the ring, silently and formally.
One after another they march
Around the ring, proudly, like men.
I stand on my toes and speak softly—
They all start to gallop at once
Noiselessly, weightlessly,
Their hoofs beating only within me.
Around the ring, faster and faster,
Their manes like flame in the moonlight,
They gallop in single file,
Halt as I think the command,
Then walk out of the ring
Into darkness, proudly and softly.
One horse only stays with me
Straining to hear a command
That I am unable to utter.
On a sign from someone unseen

The jumps rise up into place
By themselves, hugely and suddenly.
The horse kneels down on the grass
And rises up with a rider.
As I watch from my place as a judge
My heart and my bones leave my body
And are heart and bones of this rider.
As the horse flies over the fences
The horseman whose heart is the judge's
Makes no movement or sound,
But the horse knows what he must do
And he takes the fences one by one
Not touching the poles or the ground.
At the end of the course he halts
And the fences retreat to the ringside,
Then my horse and his rider are gone.
Alone in the grandstand's shadow
I call to him time after time
But only my bones fill my body.
The rider and horse do not answer.
I walk across to the gate
Looking back once more at the ring
Watching for sound or a movement
Left behind by one horse that I love.
The empty ring does not echo
And the horse has left no hoofprints.
In the moonlight, alone, I sink down
Kneeling in nothing but bones
And I call to my horse once again
But the ring and the grandstand are quiet.

II *The Horse*

In the darkened stable I move in my sleep
And my hoof stirs the straw and wakes me.
I rise, breathing softly, inhaling
The moonlight outside like perfume,
Straining to hear the command
That moved my hoof in the straw.

In my huge, shining shape I stand
Listening, and I hear the calling again.
Through the locked door of my stall,
Obeying, I march to the show ring,
Beside horses I cannot see, but feel
As their hoofs shake the air around me.
I march to the sound of a heart
That beats somewhere just ahead of me.
In the ring I lead a parade
In a circle, galloping and galloping,
And I wait for a change in the heartbeat.
I halt, and the others march out,
And I sink to my knees on the grass
As a body gets up on my back
And the man in the ring disappears.
I rise to my feet once again
And look around me at fences
Which have sprung like trees from the ground.
My shape fills the air as I fly
Over boards, stone walls, and poles,
And the bones on my back do not move.
Still I move to the beat of a heart
That brought me out of the stable.
I stop when I clear the last fence,
And the bones dismount, and I march
From the ring to the sound of the heart.
Back in my stable I lie down
Wide-eyed, breathless and shining,
Still hearing within me the call
That brought me over the jumps.
This time I cannot obey:
This man is only partly a rider
And the rider in him is within me.
Helpless, grief-stricken, and alone,
He kneels out there in the moonlight
With only his bones for a body,
His heart singing deeply within
A shape that moves with new life.
I believe in the singing, and sleep.

And so no force, however great, can stretch a
cord, however fine, into a horizontal line
which shall be absolutely straight.
—William Whewell, Elementary Treatise on
Mechanics *(1819)*

AN AFTERNOON OF
POCKET BILLIARDS

I
Breakings

Breakings

Long before I first left home, my father
tried to teach me horses, land, and sky,
to show me how his kind of work was done.
I studied how to be my father's son,
but all I learned was, when the wicked die,
they ride combines through barley forever.

Every summer I hated my father
as I drove hot horses through dusty grass;
and so I broke with him, and left the farm
for other work, where unfamiliar weather
broke on my head an unexpected storm
and things I had not studied came to pass.

So nothing changes, nothing stays the same,
and I have returned from a broken home
alone, to ask for a job breaking horses.
I watch a colt on a long line making
tracks in dust, and think of the kinds of breakings
there are, and the kinds of restraining forces.

Goodbye to the Old Friends

Because of a promise I cannot break
I have returned to my father's house, and here,
for the first time in years, I have risen
early this Sunday to visit the Friends.
As I drive to the Meeting House, the trees
wave softly as the wind moves over me.

I am late. Faces turn to look at me;
I sit in a pew apart, and silence breaks
slightly, like the rustle of old trees.
I wonder whether I am welcome here,
but in the old wall clock I see a friend.
An old man I remember now has risen

to say that this is Easter. Christ has risen.
The ticking of the old wall clock distracts me
as this old man addresses his friends;
he prowls for an hour through a Bible, breaks
his voice to bring my wandering mind back here
from aimless circling through the aging trees

whose branches tick like clocks. Boughs cut from trees,
disposed through the room, remind me of the risen
Christ this voice speaks of; I do not see him here.
I do not see him here, but flowers tell me,
on the mantel before us, in scent that breaks
above the graying heads of nodding Friends,

on hats and in lapels of aging Friends,
the flowers and the branches from the trees
remind me of what this old man's voice breaks

for the last time to tell us: Christ has risen.
With the tongue of a man he speaks to me
and to his Friends: there are no angels here.

At last I shout without breath my first prayer here
and ask for nothing but silence. Two old Friends
turn slowly toward each other, letting me
know how much silence remains. The trees
ripple the silence, and the spirit has risen.
Two old hands of marble meet and Meeting breaks.

Old Friends move over the lawn, among old trees.
One offers me his hand. I have risen,
I am thinking, as I break away from here.

Girl with a Flute

for Ann Cherry

She appeared, and there were no
words spoken. She stood with
her back and her long blond
hair to the wall, as,

in the days of heroes,
stone women by the score
held on their patient heads
the roofs of Grecian temples.

Time goes by, and on
those isles, the wind has blown
their stone clothes thin; but now,
upon a sign ceremoniously

given, she sits with her
wide skirt around her, takes
up with care the silver
flute, and moves as no one

ever has, and makes such sounds
as men, as men are now,
have never heard before.
The music stops; she bows,

walks to the door and rises
slowly, smiling, through the air,
playing the Haydn Flute Concerto
as she rides the wind away.

Long Distance

You ask me if I think you do not care
And I shall say some words to the receiver
And fear they will not be the words you hear:
I cannot lay my hand upon your shoulder.

December Love Song

Outside the diner, snow
   muffles the lighted street.
You sit before me now,
and I, through smoke and steam,
   stare at your lips, repeat
not yours, but words I dream
   you send above the chink
   of forks and plates. I shrink,

become a boy of eight
   perched on a washing machine:
close to our inadequate
and antiquated radio,
   I dream my ears as keen
as those of stern-lipped Tonto
   warning the Lone Ranger
   of imperceptible danger.

All my childish wishes
   concentrate on static,
the clatter of the dishes
in the sink before my mother,
   the roar of the automatic
washing machine, all other
   disruptive sounds that can
   drown out the tall Masked Man

and the Indian, the sounds
   from good and bad guys' guns.
My heart is out of bounds
now, beyond the swinging door,

beyond the cinnamon buns
untouched on the plate before
    your eyes that try to reach
    beyond attempts at speech,

back with the drum of hooves,
    the note of recognition—
as the White Horse Silver moves
across the plain, following
    the wind and the donation
of the Bullet—in the bellowing
    of one proud man who knows
    the Masked Man and tells those

who wondered who this was
    whose ringing voice is dying
now. Outside, the snow is
falling on the street, on eyes,
    the White Horse Silver, lying
on lips, your voice that tries
    to reach across this table, where
    it dies, drowned out in static air.

Goodbye to the Goya Girl

Woman with a Scarf

When we were formally introduced
I was expected to doubt
that you could speak through that glass.
She had no reason to suspect
that you were the best of backbiters.

The way you used that glass was like a woman,
holding it so carefully between us,
the finishing touch to your face.

I fell for your eyes and mouth, your voice
most of all. I wanted even those arms
around me, and they were.

Divorce

He travels fastest who travels alone,
And he kills two birds with one rolling stone.

Among the Departures from This House

In Coke bottles waiting to be returned,
under the faded couch, beside the bed,
in empty cups which perch about the room,

dust settles, gathers, breeds, and comes alive.
It grows like snow—nothing improves before
the slow and tactless onslaught of my hands,

until, as I lie sifting toward sleep,
the little balls of dust unite, fall in,
move out like lemmings, marching against the wind.

An Afternoon of Pocket Billiards

Here where there is neither hope nor haste
all my days blend; each dark day is misplaced
　　　　inside my crowded head.
I try to beat a game, half chance, half cold
and steady practice, struggling for the skill
that might kill chance. But chance's claws take hold,
the game is wrecked, and time is all I kill:
no sleight of hand or heart can overcome
the fear that, in this darkness, only time
　　　　is not already dead.

I narrow down my gaze to where I waste
days growing used to a dusty taste
　　　　that hangs in the dead air;
motes of chalk and talcum powder sift
down past the hard edge of the swinging light
above my table. Jukebox voices drift
by me through the dark, raveled with a slight
vibration from that older world beyond
the window: now I listen for a sound
　　　　that may still rise somewhere

　　　　this afternoon, away
from here . . . my eyes wander from where I play
to the motions of more skillful hands than mine:
another player leans above his cue.
Between us, those old tremors seem to move
the air I stare through, almost as if you
were breathing here: that half-remembered love
　　　　obscures the perfect shot
I turned to watch; I turn back, but am caught
between my past and the shifting design

on a green field of order where I wait
for time and strength of will to dissipate
            these shapes that coil and turn
above the hush and click of herded spheres.
Brief glimpses of a chain of treacheries
flicker around a melody that bears
into this room the gradual disease
we fled when you tore blindly out our driveway
for the last time, and I came here to play,
            to wait for your return,

for this game's random shifts to bring you back
or set me free. As I blunder through each rack,
            no two shots are the same;
yet if, beneath them all, dim certainties
evolve to hold my called shots on a course
that weaves beyond love's sudden vagaries,
still, an impulse like love, in the force
behind that wavering song, caroms my thought
into an old mistake: with every shot
            I call, I speak your name.

High and low, striped and solid balls rotate
in endless formations as time grows late.
            My concentration breaks
just at the dead-reckoned instant before
each shot: testing stroke and angle, I ease
down on the felt and line it up once more;
too late, I feel that slight vibration seize
my arm—too late to stand. My knocking heart
shatters skill and chance, and takes the game apart.
            I make my own mistakes.

I chalk my cue and call for one more rack,
believing I might still untwist the wreck
            your song makes in my head.
I think how spellbound Bottom woke to shout
through nightmare trees, "When my cue comes, call me,
and I will answer . . ." Your voice might find me out,

note by note unraveling to recall me
from this enchanted wood beyond your reach.
"When my cue comes . . ." Moving only by touch,
    I try to hold the thread,

listening for the words to an old song
that draws me down, sets me adrift among
    patterns below the game.
The words will not connect. Red blood and bone,
older than love, the swirling echo drives
me down below green felt toward solid stone
whose grains read out the sequence of my lives
in sounds like underwater footsteps. My blind
and whispering fingers stroke the stone to find
    strength to forget the shame

I learned too long ago. I may be wrong
to follow an ancient, dimly-sounding song
    whose melody is fear,
whose words might never speak; but now I know
that in it, somewhere, forces of hand and will
combine like dancers on a stage. And now,
within the strictness of my touch, I feel
a surge of steadiness. I rise to air,
to dust and vacant noise and old despair.
    Error still holds me here,

    but I'll be right someday:
though one song of old love has died away,
an older song is falling into place.
From now on I will play to make it speak,
to see the form its words give to this game.
I see, as I move into another rack,
that all days in this cavern are the same:
    endless struggles to know
how cold skill and a force like love can flow
together in my veins, and be at peace.

Here where there is neither hope nor haste
I narrow down my gaze to where I waste
      this afternoon away;
on a green field of order, where I wait
for this game's random shifts to bring you back,
high and low, striped and solid balls rotate.
I chalk my cue and call for one more rack,
listening for the words to an old song
I learned too long ago: "I may be wrong,
      but I'll be right someday."

The Hughesville Scythe

The hills where I grew up had learned to hide
destructions from each other long before
Hughesville saw destruction take its store,
and still the Hughesville legend has not died:

how once the storekeeper unlocked the door
to find he had been robbed. One clue, beside
the hearth, a swallow's nest on the stone floor,
told him how the burglar had got inside.

The old man took a scythe-blade from his store
and fixed it in the chimney, across the fine-
edged dark, where it would split a man who tried
to come that way again and steal his gold.

No burglar ever came. Now those designs
are choked in honeysuckle, and the old
insistent rituals of decay unfold:
yet in my brain that unused blade still shines,

and when I try to walk through dark I hold
my hand before me, touching solid signs,
thinking how a man can hunt for gold
and lie in pieces in the raging vines.

II

*Learning to
Face Extinction*

Pastoral

for David R. Slavitt

In the country, you learn to live at peace
with your neighbor; he is farther away,
but when you meet, you always stop and talk.

You learn that he is a pathologist
who every day kisses his wife goodbye
and goes to the lab, and blows up a goat.

The trees grow up around you as he speaks.

Afterwards, he counts the fragments, notes
their average size, and calculates the impact
with which they struck the walls.
                              In the evening,
you might hear him mowing his lawn, or closing
his garage door for the night. Cricket sounds
surround you both out here; in the morning,
when you pass him on the road, you smile and wave.

Amazing but True

In the Chamber of Natural Curiosities,
a man cries "Fraud!" and points
at the two-headed calf, his finger tracing
what might be the seam of the taxidermist's needle
around the base of one head's neck.

One way or the other, craft or miraculous birth,
it has found its way here
to this fly-specked wood shelf. Its four plastic eyes
stare a message you can never forget: born or made,
it is something you have to believe.

Snapshot

So huge he couldn't reach below his belt
(he'd been a sideshow fat man for a while),
Mr. Shipman always kept a boy with him
whose job, whenever he was called upon,
was to unbutton that enormous fly,
reach in and grab, then stand aside and aim.
Once, behind the grandstand at a ball game,
while Shipman shifted his impatient flesh
from foot to foot, the boy groped in the trousers
and said, "Mr. Shipman, I can't find it." "Well,
God damn it, boy, you the last man had it."

Riding Lesson

I learned two things
from an early riding teacher.
He held a nervous filly
in one hand and gestured
with the other, saying, "Listen.
Keep one leg on one side,
the other leg on the other side,
and your mind in the middle."

He turned and mounted.
She took two steps, then left
the ground, I thought for good.
But she came down hard, humped
her back, swallowed her neck,
and threw her rider as you'd
throw a rock. He rose, brushed
his pants and caught his breath,
and said, "See, that's the way
to do it. When you see
they're gonna throw you, get off."

Campaign Promise

During the Great Debates, he tried a joke
and nothing happened. For an instant, hatred
for everything he saw leapt from his eyes
to his mouth, and down his arm to one hand
the camera caught and held as it gripped something—
the lectern, a table's corner, I forget what—
which, had it been alive, he would have killed.

How It Looks on Paper

for Jack Vernon

The President's hands rove
lovingly over a sheet of paper.

    And right here under this tree,

As usual, here's Vietnam. That's
the Delta, of course, and

    his damp foot touching real soil,

over here, this crosshatched
area, we have Cambodia. Now

    his small ear straining for something

these small black regions here,
these kidney-shaped spots

    that even in this place sounds wrong,

on the border, these are pockets
of resistance (see illustration).

    wondering what is about to emerge

If some of the men stationed
in this white part of the page

    from the heavy fog rolling toward him,

are moved across here into this
crosshatched sector, then we can

a boy with dark eyes waits to see

make a quick sweep, like
this, and eradicate a serious

whether his luck will hold out,

threat to the many American
lives now occupying this

and if so, where it will take him.

portion of the page, down here.

Speech

1

I crouch over my radio
to tune in the President,
thinking how lucky I am
not to own a television.

2

Now the rich, cultivated voice
with its cautious, measured pauses
fills my living room, fills
the wastebasket, the vase
on the mantel, the hurricane
lamps, and even fills
the antique pottery whiskey jug
beside the fireplace, nourishing
the dried flowers I have put in it.

3

"I had a responsibility,"
he says; the phrase pours
from the speaker like molasses,
flows to the rug, spreads
into a black, shining puddle,
slowly expands, covers
the rug with dark sweetness.
It begins to draw flies;

they eat all the syrup
and clamor for more.

4

I can barely hear the speech
above the buzzing of their wings.
But the Commander in Chief
has the solution: another
phrase, sweeter, thicker,
blacker, oozes out
over my living room floor:
"I have personal reasons
for wanting peace." This is more
than the flies will be able to eat;
they will stay quiet
for the rest of the speech.

5

Now, you are thinking, comes
the Good Part, the part
where the syrup proves poisonous
and kills all the flies.
My fellow Americans, that
is not at all what happened.
The flies grew fat on the phrases,
grew as large as bullfrogs.

6

They are everywhere in the house,
and the syrup continues
to feed and fatten them;
in the pottery whiskey jug,
sprouting new leaves and buds,
even the dried flowers thrive.

7

The speech
has been over for weeks now;
they go on eating,
but they stay quiet
and seem peaceful enough.
At night, sometimes,
I can hear them
making soft liquid sounds
of contentment.

Toad

Squat in the stagnant sunlight
on the moss beneath a shrub
its tongue slowly flicking
its throat slowly throbbing
huddled alone in the wood.
A ten-year-old boy exploring
found it damp and sparkling there
and caught it up in his hands.
He felt the frightened
water on his fingers.
Into his pocket carefully
so he could carry it home
and down on the floor he played
making it hop for his joy.
But the room was too dry
it heaved for air and died
dust clinging to its skin.
Weeping he knelt on the floor
holding this love in his fingers
waiting for someone to speak.
Before he went to bed
he put it in a box
and hid it in his closet
behind a baseball glove.

Learning to Face Extinction

STORM MOUNTAIN SLIDE AREA

I stop my car on a curve in a canyon road,
between two signs forbidding my parking here.
Above my head uncountable tons of snow
hover precariously on the mountainside.

Below me and to the west, the yellow dome
of Salt Lake City's man-made atmosphere
undulates against the upper air.
Farther up, to the east, the Rangers' cannon
topples the wavering balance on another hill.

Above my head a mountain is holding its breath.

SALT STORM

All day high winds swept in from the west,
lifting alkali and salt toward the sky,
blotting out the sun, turning the valley gray.
At nightfall, a light rain brought it all down.

This morning, people stand beside their cars
in long lines at the automatic car wash,
testing their smudged fingers on their tongues.

One by one, they ease into the dark
tunnel of nozzles and steam; the fine spray
clouds and hits the gutters toward the storm drains.

Water-beaded cars nose out into the streets,
roaring into the first clear day this spring.

THE VIEW FROM A CAB

An odd day. For the first time in years,
I am in New York. Riding in from
the airport on the bus, I have seen
abandoned cars spilling out their guts
onto loops of freeway cloverleaves.
The light looks dangerous. Anywhere else,
people would expect a hurricane:
the haze on the city has an edge,
like an inverted saucer. The sun
pries up one edge with a slanting ray.
I get in a cab. "This weather, huh?
I tell you what, it's them astronauts,
they're the cause of it." "How's that?" I say.
"I'm not sure," he says, "but I know this:
fuck with the moon, the sun don't like it."

Buildings and Grounds

for Richard Dillard

The house we moved into has been landscaped
    so that it has the portable, plastic look
    of a Sears, Roebuck toy farm.

All up and down our street, the same minor artist seems
    to have been at work; our neighbors' lawns are
    watered and mowed truly until they are carpets,

their shrubs are lovingly trimmed and shaped
    into green velvet eggs and spheres.
    Our neighbors watch us like hawks,

wondering whether we have the equipment,
    the know-how, the spirit, to strive with them
    as they strive with their landscapes.

Oh, let me bring my home from the South to this street!
    I will let the grass grow until it is knee-high,

I will import chickens and a blue-tick hound to trample
    the grass and dig bone-holes and scratch-holes,

I will set up on cinderblocks in the front yard
    a '38 Ford with no tires or headlights,

I will sit in the gutted driver's seat
    with a bottle of Old Mr. Mac, glaring at my
    neighbors, reading aloud from *God's Little Acre*,

I will be a prophet of wildness and sloth!

But the Puritan gaze of my neighbors cuts through
my desperate vision of home—my dream house
will not flourish here.

I will spend my rapidly declining years
reading the labels on bags of crabgrass killer,

pushing my lawn mower until my front yard
is as smooth as a green on a golf course,

clipping and shaping my landlord's opulent shrubs.

But don't misunderstand me—I have not been
converted; I will still make something
to sustain me here in this alien land.

I will plant mint in the flowerbeds beside
the Shasta daisies we brought from Monticello,

I will set up a croquet course on the front lawn
with a slender drink-stand at each wicket
to hold my frosty mint juleps,

I will station an iron jockey by the driveway
to stare back into the pitiless eyes
of my neighbors' pink plastic flamingoes,

I will keep a Tennessee Walking Horse in the garage
and give him a foxhound for company,

I will stand out front in a white linen suit
surveying my plantation,

I will plant a magnolia tree.

But now, at the height of my visionary ecstasy,
the telephone rings. It is the man
next door, calling to let me know

that my sprinkler is turned up too high
    and is sprinkling the seats of his convertible.

I go out to turn down the water, and I see
    that the cedar needs trimming again,
    that the elm twigs need to be raked.

I will do those things. I will hoe and trench
    and weed, I will mow the grass.
    I have moved in here now,

and I have to do what I can.

III
From Porlock

The Writer-in-Residence Discusses His Working Habits

I often compose in my head
while working outside,
raking leaves or mowing the lawn
or feeding azaleas. Leaves
have sogged on my lawn
through two snows now.

———

I used to write with a fountain pen,
not typing until I had written
several longhand drafts.
But at my present level of fame
my books reach the galley-proof stage
without my having written a word.

———

Electricity furnishes
power for my lamp,
my cigarette lighter,
my pencil sharpener,
my typewriter,
and both of my tape recorders.

———

This piece of equipment
is a Veeder-Root counter.
It fits in the hand
like this, the thumb
poised on the button.
I count my words with it,
which requires concentration

since my rhythmical habit
is to count syllables.

———

I slip my wastepaper
into the basket
still flat,
in an upright stack.
If I crumple it,
it lies there uncrumpling
with a sound
between ticking and whispering.

———

The men in that photograph?
One is myself, somewhat
younger than I am now;
the other is Faulkner
or Stevens or Pound . . .
you can see from his expression
what good friends we were.

———

I have three calendars:
one above my desk
for decoration;
one in my pocket
for lectures and reading engagements;
and one in my filing cabinet
for the deaths of literary figures.

De Gustibus Ain't What Dey Used to Be

Poetry, like the old darky mowing the lawn, can't be hurried.
  —Marshall Fishwick

You have to know how to handle it.
Treated with understanding,
it is loyal, slow, and dependable,
with an earthy charm of its own.
  It walks into your life and sits down.

If it sometimes moves so sluggishly
that the grass grows up behind it
as fast as it's being cut,
you tell it to keep trying.
  It will not be hurried.

It shuffles and makes excuses
and tells you the mower is dull,
but you know better than that:
never trust it with machinery.
  It makes room for itself in your life.

It breaks everything it touches,
and steals what isn't nailed down;
its speech is a savage mumble,
and it lies just to keep in practice.
  There are things it will force you to see.

It promises to come back next week,
but you know it probably won't;
it is liable to get its throat cut
by another one just like it.
  It has settled on your life for good.

It shambles over the lawn
taking its own sweet time.
It can never be overworked;
it has a natural rhythm.
    It will stay. It will finally own you.

The New York Poet

So its the old lady mostly gets me down
these last few weeks
I mean a man has to take things easy
after a long day
stretch out
take off his shoes
watch some tv
                    maybe
drink a few beers evenins

& the old lady   what the hell
she know about it anyway
shes on my back
the minute she gets home
from the library
arms full of old paper bags
gum wrappers all thru her hair
she wants to know what the hell
I been doin   I tell her
I been trying to keep body
& soul together   keep
her fat clothes on her fat ass

See them hands   shit
you dont think you get hands like that
on yr butt in front a tv
all the time   I work
like a sonofabitch all day
skin my knuckles trying to straighten
secondhand frames   stringin
old wires across em   one thing & another

like to break my freakin back
hangin out 21st story windows the whole
damn day talkin to pilots & pigeons

I mean   a man has his work to do
but evenins   he wants to take
things easy
                    jesus
just lookit them freakin hands

Three Small Seizures

> *Every writer I know*
> *hates other writers. Not all others, but most.*
> *The ones who are better or different he has to hate*
> *because they are better or different.*
> *And those who are worse*
> *he despises because that is his earned right.*
> —David R. Slavitt,
> The Eclogues of Virgil

INTERVIEW

"Why so pale and wan?"
said Rod McKuen to Kahlil Gibran;
"Your graffiti have darkened my desperate ruin,"
said Kahlil Gibran to Rod McKuen.

ON A POSTHUMOUS BOOK OF POEMS

These pages bring to mind, as I flip through
the efforts of the more-than-once-removed,
the poet's painful search for flawlessness:
what should not have survived an early purge
lies here as if it had the breath to bless
a hand that had no better work to do
than shuffling through a dead man's trash to forge
a corpus which a corpse might have improved.

TO AN OLDER POET

Young for my years, impertinent, perhaps
a poet and perhaps not—so you said.
I remind you, in a momentary lapse
of taste, that when I'm your age you'll be dead.

Pineapples Since 1500

for Chippy Howe, who, on a night when she and all her classmates were hysterically studying for a history exam, called me to say that she could not draw pineapples.

Dates pass before my eyes, names,
dates, wars, discoveries, crowned heads,
and dates. They are not numbers
to me any more, but men and wars
and discoveries and names.
The wind howls at my window,
men march outside from down
the road, making war, discoveries,
dates. It is useless. I take up
my pen, my pad, attempt a bear
or two; too small and simple,
on the whole. A fruit or two—
a date—no, not a fruit like that.
A pineapple. Surmounted by
a crown of leaves, it sits, too round,
too crosshatched to be believed.
Another. Too tall and narrow; the edges
look like edges. Zig-Zag? No.
The leaves don't look right, either.
An apple? A pine? Thin, red, tall,
green and round. Not so fat as that,
nameless kings and princes march
through my mind, ships on seas uncharted
sail to forgotten lands where perfect
pineapples await the sailors
as they steer their boats to shores
I can't remember, can't forget;
men march and halt and march in print
and leave me here with dreams of bears
among the ripe pineapples, though
the wind howls and time marches
in a double column, double time.

Another Message from Porlock

hark to the musical clank
   —Walt Whitman

Toward Main Hall at the upper end of the quad,
as evening comes on, the literary gathering begins.
Going in, we can hear down the length of the veranda
the clatter of dinner dishes beginning to subside
in the kitchen. We trickle in to the Green Drawing Room,
browsing a moment among the few plush chairs reserved
for the handful of dignified regulars. Most of us
sit on the floor. Soon we take up the ritual signaling,
collecting in groups of friends who can make one ashtray
suffice, like a multiplied loaf. We settle down
for the introduction.
                  The poetry suits us. Here,
almost no one could seem far out of place; we welcome
what comes. Two poems to start, then a small joke;
we chuckle; we are friends. Growing deeper into himself,
he turns to his darker side, unraveling the energy
he builds toward his real platform pieces. Our breath
tightens; he carries us on a surf of words, on now
to his favorite, the long one we who are with him can follow.
Yet some of us glance at our watches, remembering
that even here a few things can arrive on schedule:

A sharp tap begins it; the listeners stiffen,
stop hearing the words of the poem. The ashtrays hang
in mid-pass: we all know what happens next.
Spang in the middle of a pivotal stanza,
the pipes in the walls fill with water and steam.
At first we try to ignore it, but none of us can:
we have been here before, and know what to expect.
Like a percolator picking up speed, the clamor
increases, and pauses, and then increases again
with a drunken battering, hissing, and thumping,

so that even the silences between pipeknocks have all
our attention, whether or not the poet proceeds.
Some of us wonder if we remember a pattern
in the way the banging climbs to a petulant stillness
that is filled, for a while, with our fears
that it probably will not last.
                              But it does,
and the poet is still reading on, having flinched
only once, more to acknowledge our embarrassment
than to register his. We settle again, and light up,
seeing silence redeemed by intrusion, silence
made ready at last to receive his hard-earned words.

To Hear My Head Roar

First, my father taught me to read poetry
aloud; then my teachers in grade school
remembered how he had recited poetry,

how many times he had brought down the school-
house with "Casey at the Bat." Whenever they
could they called me up before the whole school

to be my father's son. I still dream of days they
stood me shaking before my classmates, then
waited while I launched into what they

knew from long experience was coming, then
sat through "Jabberwocky" or "Excelsior"—that was
the full range of my repertory then.

Later I almost liked it, though I was
still forced to it: each week we all recited
at assembly. A terrible, tiring time that was

for my audience, and for me, as I recited
"The Highwayman" and "The Cremation of
Sam McGee." My father coached as I recited

nightly in the living room, and on the day of
my graduation from that place, my sister
and I recited, respectively, "The Ballad of

the Harp-Weaver" and "The Highwayman." My sister
and I fled to our father's side after
it was over, and I can still see my sister

blushing as the old ladies came up after
the performance with tears in their eyes
to tell my father we were wonderful. After

that, it was a long time before my eyes
would follow the tricks of poems, but now I know
dozens of them: they unscroll behind my eyes,

and I own hundreds of books in which I know
I can always find the right thing at the right time,
and I will read to anyone who doesn't know

what he is in for, for hours at a time.
When I try to understand this part of myself,
I think back to that earlier, troublesome time

to find that the explanation of myself
does not lie there entirely; for now I recall being
in high school, just beginning to take myself

seriously, and my father as a human being,
and I think of hours I spent in the attic
rummaging through old file cases, being

surprised to find, in the dark dust of that attic,
the poems my father had written when he
was in college. One afternoon in the attic

yielded an ancient treasure, a recording he
had once made and then forgotten. I
tiptoed out of the attic with it, thinking he

might take it from me, and secretly I
tried it, at first without success, on the machine
downstairs in the living room. At last I

even tried to start the reluctant machine
on the inner end of the groove. It worked.
The thing had been cut on some amateur's machine

and was made to run from the inside out. I worked
with the needle, nudging it over the cracks,
and heard, after what seemed hours of work,

a voice that I recognized, through dusty cracks
and thirty years, as my father's (or my own), say
something I now take to heart as my heart cracks:

"This is Tom Taylor talking; talking," I heard him say,
"to hear his own voice, and reading some poetry
because he wants to have something to say."

IV
Harvest

Riding a One-Eyed Horse

One side of his world is always missing.
You may give it a casual wave of the hand
or rub it with your shoulder as you pass,
but nothing on his blind side ever happens.

Hundreds of trees slip past him into darkness,
drifting into a hollow hemisphere
whose sounds you will have to try to explain.
Your legs will tell him not to be afraid

if you learn never to lie. Do not forget
to turn his head and let what comes come seen:
he will jump the fences he has to if you swing
toward them from the side that he can see

and hold his good eye straight. The heavy dark
will stay beside you always; let him learn
to lean against it. It will steady him
and see you safely through diminished fields.

Smoking in Bed in the Fire Chief's House

A gull drops clams on rocks
near where I lie taking what sun
there is above Nantucket, lulled almost
to sleep by the sound of waves, kept
awake by the thud of clams

on sand, and the rattling
sigh of salt-grass on the moors.
As the gull rises and falls, flickering in
and out of the corner of my eye,
the beach becomes the sheet

of my rented bed in town,
held as if by a ring of men. In a dull
daze between sleep and waking, I think the sheet
is slackened and pulled taut by hunters
in the north—they toss the gull,

the lightest hunter, high
into the air, so that from his perch
on nothing he can search for the blowhole
of the seal, the shifting whiteness
of the polar bear.

Closer to sleep, I become
the sharp-eyed hunter, tossed from the blanket
in time with waves; I rise above, then fall
below the gull, who hangs motionless
in the air beyond the rail

of the rolling ferry
that brought me here; he drifts
in and out of my field of vision as the boat
rocks slowly over the waves, lifting
me out of troughs, above

the waves, to look toward
the land I fled, as it recedes
into the distance beyond the stationary gull,
before I am caught, let down, then tossed
again to train my eyes

on the land beyond the shore,
to search out the quarry, whatever
it was I fled when I embarked. Driving
down the gangplank from the parking hold,
I carry glimpses of the world

I left behind—a face,
a cold flame around my heart, burning
images reduced to ash by time and distance:
glimpses that will fade, then blaze up,
as I drive to my rented room

in Irving Bartlett's house.
His wife shows me where things are; she points
at last to a brass gong above my bedroom door.
"It rings," she says, "whenever there's
a fire. My husband is

the Fire Chief here." So far,
it has clattered every day, only
to let the whole town know the noon hour
has arrived—there has been no alarm
set off by burning house

or tree, or by the flame
I cannot kindle in my brain.
Here nothing burns—not even my pale skin

in the slant sunlight. I pray
for sparks, but nothing catches fire

inside me or around me
as I ride the sounds of gulls and waves
to sleep, to dream myself astride a borrowed horse,
riding across the moors, listening
for gabbling beagles smoking

over a scent laid down
by hares. Beneath the horse's hooves
soft sand gives way along the beach where I lie
asleep, dreaming now of lying awake
with a lighted cigarette

in the Fire Chief's house,
thinking how the room might blaze around me
if I should fall asleep—how a fire might catch
hold of me once more, to wrap me
in tongues until my voice

could sing a name for the face
that chars within me. A *clack* beside
my head snaps me awake; I throw the broken
clam away, out over a rail that blurs
as sleep recedes toward

the shore I cannot see.
Awake at last, I watch this land
shine from the waves for the first time since I came.
The face I fled is ashes now,
and I can love the gull

who drops toward the clam
I threw out over moors where beagles
blaze over the trail of the hare, their voices
ringing in my ears, mingling with
the fire bell and the waves

until their flaming tongues
fill the air above the moors with song.
The face I wanted to name becomes this landscape,
named forever only by the sea.
My tongue on fire at last,

I rise from this beach,
turning toward the flame-touched song
of hounds. Under their smoking breath, in the wind,
the salt-grass burns on the sand
dunes, blade by blade.

Harvest

Every year in late July I come back to where I was raised,
   to mosey and browse through old farm buildings,
   over fields that seem never to change,

rummaging through a life I can no longer lead
   and still cannot leave behind, looking for relics
   which might spring back to that life at my touch.

Today, among thistles and ragweed, I stumble on
   a discarded combine—the old kind we pulled
   with a tractor to cut and thresh barley and wheat.

Now it lies listing into the side of this hill
   like a stone or an uprooted stump, harboring snakes
   and wasps, rusting slowly down into the briars.

Still, I climb to the seat, wondering whether it will
   hold me, fumbling for pedals and levers
   I used to know by heart. Above my head,

the grain-pipe forks down to the bag-clamps,
   and a wad of tie-strings, gone weedy and rotten,
   still hangs by my right hand. As I touch these things,

this machine I once knew by many unprintable names
   moves out through barley in late July, and the stalks
   fall to the knife as the paddle-reel sweeps them in.

On wide canvas belts, cut grain rides into the dark
   insides of the combine, where frantic shakers and screens
   break the grain loose from the stalks and the chaff;

almost invisible, small spines from the grain-heads
   pour out through holes in the metal, billowing
   into a cloud that moves with us over the hills,

engulfing me, the machine, the tractor and driver,
   as we work in a spiral to the center of the field,
   rolling back through the years in a dust cloud.

The spines stick to my skin, work into my pores,
   my bloodstream, and finally blaze into my head
   like a miniature cactus of hatred for all grain,

for flour and cereal and bread, for mildewed surplus
   swelling in midwestern silos. Never again,
   I thought once, as I rode out the cloud until sundown,

never again. I climb down and walk out through the thistles,
   still breathing fifteen-year-old barley. The years
   in the cloud drift back to me. Metal rusts into the hill.

Barley-dust pricks at my brain, and I am home.

Canticle of Created Things

from the Italian of San Francesco d'Assisi

Thine be the praise, good Lord
omnipotent, most high, Thine
the honor, the glory, and every blessing.
To Thee alone, most high, do these belong;
to speak Thy name no living man is worthy.

Be praised, my Lord, with all that Thou hast made;
above all else the sun, our master and our brother,
whence Thy gift of daylight comes.
He is most fair, and radiant with great splendor,
and from Thee, most high, his meaning comes.

Be praised, my Lord, for our sister moon,
    and for the stars;
Thou hast placed in the heavens their clear
    and precious beauty.
Be praised, my Lord, for our brother wind
and for the air, in all weathers cloudy and clear,
whence comes sustenance for all which Thou hast made.

Be praised, my Lord, for our sister water,
who is most useful, precious, humble and pure.

Be praised, my Lord, for our brother fire,
for Thine is the power by which he lights the dark;
Thine are his beauty and joy, his vigor and strength.

Be praised, my Lord, for earth, our mother
    and our sister;
by Thy power she sustains and governs us,
and puts forth fruit in great variety, with grass
    and colorful flowers.

Be praised, my Lord, for those who forgive
   by the power of Thy love within them,
for those who bear infirmities and trials;
blessed are those who endure in peace,
for Thou at last shalt crown them, O most high.

Be praised, my Lord, for our sister bodily death,
from whom no living man escapes;
woe unto those who die in mortal sin,
but blessed be those whom death shall find
   living by Thy most sacred wishes,
for through the second death no harm
   shall come to them.

Praise my Lord and give thanks unto Him;
bless my Lord and humbly serve Him.

Burning a Horse

We watch him burn—
          hoof, hide, and bone.
     —James Seay

Riding on a flatbed wagon, carrying with us
    an ax, pitchforks, a coil of heavy rope,
    and a five-gallon can of kerosene,

we went to the back meadow that afternoon,
    driven to desperate measures
    by the stench that hung on the still air,

dead air that lay like fog in the valley
    around us, not enough motion in it even
    to carry buzzards whose random glide

might have brought them to the body
    of the Percheron that festered on the grass
    where we had dragged him after he had died.

We spent an hour cutting brush from fallen trees,
    carrying it to where the horse lay bulging
    in the sun; we hooked him to the tractor

and pulled him over the pile of brush,
    to get it under him, then soaked
    the brushpile and his body with the kerosene.

I threw a match into the trembling vapors
    that rose from the fuel and from the rotting
    horse, then dropped back as the explosion

blasted us with the smell of burning hair. Slowly,
    one patch of skin, then another, burned through
    to let the gas escape and blaze like a blowtorch,

but the flames died down too soon, and we could hear
    the flesh speaking, one of the men said, as
    a cornfield does, growing after a hard rain.

We ran up to the pyre with more brush, holding
    our breath as we used pitchforks to place
    the dry sticks where they seemed needed most,

and then saw fire catch the wood, the flesh,
    and saw black smoke so thick and heavy
    that it hid us from each other; it crawled

down the meadow a few feet above the ground,
    the smell we held our breath against
    tainting everything it touched. Burning at last,

the horse was blackening and shrinking into the tall
    meadow grass; and then, before us, there,
    from coals that had caught hold in the horse's bones,

we saw a horse, made whole, with heavy flesh
    and shining skin, rippling against the pull,
    rising from the grass around the dying fire,

his new hoofs shod, his mane flying, rising
    from the coals and moving in a smooth
    and dangerous way; he traveled down the meadow

at a sweeping gallop, wrapped in something
    like a flame, light and heat around him
    that did not flicker or drop from him as he disappeared.

The sun rolled down the hill above the meadow,
    and in the dusk a wind came up.
    We strained our eyes, but the horse was gone,

moving perhaps beyond the stand of willow trees
    at the upper end of the meadow, carrying
    the light around him into darkness beyond our view.

We turned to look at the spot where the fire
   had been, listening for the crackling
   of smoldering bones, but all we heard

was our own blood and breath, and the sound
   of the wind that must have carried him away. Ashes
   lifted slowly in that wind, like heavy wings.

Below Carvin's Cove

for Clarice Short

On a slope in deep woods below the dam,
I sat with a bird's voice cupped in my hands.
At my breath, a drumming chuckle rolled out
into the trees across the small ravine.

Again. I heard him answer back, and held
my breath, shifting to a crouch beside a tree,
moving one inch at a time to let the blood
flow tingling back into my deadened legs.

Then between the leaves of a sumac bush
I saw his blue head move. I laid my cheek
against the stock and watched his colors change
the woods and touch the barrels of my gun.

Between us a narrow stream trickled on stone,
invisible under thirty feet of fog
that lined the bottom of the draw like smoke
poured out of a bottle. Its edges lapped
the trunks of oaks, and ghosts of chestnut trees
as white as bones stood rooted in that cloud.

The turkey drummed again; my finger tensed
too late: I saw him break into a run
straight down the hill toward me, leap to air,
then coast in a spiral downward, like a leaf,

free-falling toward the flowing cloud below,
skimming it, whipping up feathery wisps.
Downstream he sank for good. Above his wings
the fog heaved once and then lay still again.

I caught my breath and turned to look at leaves
that glowed where he had touched them with his wings;
my gun still pointed at the sumac bush
where I last saw him standing still. Far off,
I heard a voice like his, and cupped my hands.

My Grandfather Works in His Garden

My grandfather works in his garden today.
The death that grows inside him draws him there
to struggle with the death that takes away
the only thing he keeps against despair.

He sees me at the gate and comes to talk.
He leans against a post. His eyes go small
as he stares past me at a flower-stalk.
The years rise up between us like a wall.

I say it is too hot for him. He shifts
his weight toward me, but his eyes aim still
beyond me. Then they change: the barrier lifts,
disclosing shapes that I can only feel.

As his eyes change I am a boy once more,
and seem to see him straighten as one day
he straightened when a man came to our door
to tell him that our bull had got away,

that someone ought to go and bring him back.
I hear myself asking him not to go,
but as I speak I feel my voice fall slack,
reminding me that he already knew

the way love sometimes will not let you keep
a man from dangers that he knows are there.
I watch him now as he goes down the steep
porch steps and out the lane. For hours I stare

at where I saw him last. The window-glass,
when he returns, dissolves to let me break
from here to where the bull stands eating grass.
I watch the old man wave a stick and speak

to urge him up the lane, but when the bull
turns and stands like stone, I become one
with my grandfather, before a standing-still
I cannot see him try to face alone.

A hand grows tighter on the hickory cane.
The bull walks toward a man who seems at once
to stand inside behind a window pane
and out here in the path of that advance.

I stand alone. I raise my cane up high
and put my weight into swinging down
to stop the march of that unblinking eye.
Hickory snaps across a head of stone.

The head comes on until it strikes my chest
and I fall back between those heavy hooves
and close my eyes: now I am slowly pressed
into the ground as the great bull's weight moves

to his head. I feel my grandfather's breath
go slowly out of me. I brace my thumbs
for one inspired last move: I clench my teeth
against my whistling blood, my whole head hums—

my hands move upward toward the bull's round eyes.
I shove my thumbs in deep when I have found them,
and just before the bull begins to rise
I feel his eyelids closing tight around them.

My breath comes back with the window as the bull
gets to his feet and blindly moves away.
Until he is out of sight my grandfather lies still,
then rises slowly and slowly makes his way

toward me. I run out to meet him at the gate
he leans against. Green garden fills the space
rising behind him as he shifts his weight
and tells me it is hot. I touch his face.

Miss Creighton

was still, somewhere in her seventies, among
   the last and toughest of the singlehanded
   farmers in the country around our house.

In the wind, her long blue dress would ripple
   and snap about her high-top shoes, as she rode
   her hayrake hard behind her two black Percherons.

One day, years ago, we stood at the gate
   and watched her working the field
   half a mile away;

and when she saw us, she lifted the rake-teeth,
   waved and yelled, whirled
   the long black reins above her head,

and sent those heavy horses over the hills
   toward us at a lumbering run—her blue sleeves

luffed like sails, the rake's steel wheels
   touched the ground only once in a while.

At the gate, she gazed toward where she'd been,
   and as she rolled her words
   across the air between us,

Scotland's dark blue hills took shape upon those
   fields where she worked alone to raise her beef,
   to clear her hilly land of rocks.

"It does good where I pick them up," she said,
   "and where I put them down."

Today, the last black Angus has been sold,
   the last stray stone has found its place.

Her Percherons, unharnessed now, walk side by side
   across the fields, toward what rose
   whenever she spoke:

they lean together for the last time into the pull,
   moving away from us
   over the dark blue hills of Scotland.

In Memoriam

from the Italian of Giuseppe Ungaretti

His name was
Mohammed Sceab

A descendant
of the emirs of the nomads
he killed himself
because he no longer had
a homeland

He loved France
and changed his name

He became Marcel
but he was not French
and he forgot
how to live
in the tents of his people
where they listen to choruses
of the Koran
and sip coffee

And he forgot
how to set loose
the song
of his abandonment

I went with him
and the woman who owned the hotel
where we lived
in Paris
from number 5, rue des Carmes
a faded descending alley

He rests
in the graveyard at Ivry
a suburb which
always
seems like the last day
of a broken-down carnival

And perhaps I alone
still know
that he lived

An Old Rhodes Scholar

for Arthur Kyle Davis, Jr.

Holding seminars at bay
with stern requirements and sly questioning
    grows dull as days grow longer; spring
brings back an earlier time. Thoughts go astray.

He finds himself gazing
beyond the aging trees outside his window
    at a man his friends no longer know,
a strong-armed youth poised at the end of a blazing

playing field, stretching, warming
up, pacing off the runway, his tape-wound
    bamboo pole beside him on the ground.
So long ago. He blinks to shake off swarming

visions that always return
to catch him napping: he lifts the vaulting pole
    toward the bar, begins to roll
forward on his left foot to start his run.

Slowly the upper end
of the pole descends toward the mark
    and he is raised in a sunlit arc
to the trembling bar. He hoists his feet, bends

his waist, then hangs, jack-
knife, above the sawdust pit for an instant
    too perfect for the crowd of distant
admirers to believe, straightens his back,

then, like a cruising bird
that hunts for miles with hungry eyes to find
     a furred or feathered something on the ground
and finally dives on widespread unheard

     wings to earth, descends
to stand once more before these youthful faces.
     He fumbles with his notes, retraces
his steps, once more begins what never ends

     until those early days
return, unbidden, to interrupt a lecture
     on Wordsworth or the architecture
of an ode by Keats. Once more he turns away

     toward the window, pride
trembling in his voice as he recalls
     some old contest. The classroom falls
away to let us see him pausing, dignified,

     immaculate in tweeds,
his old-fashioned bamboo pole in his hands,
     ready to begin his run. He stands
a moment, thinking, then his right foot leads

     him toward the bar again,
while we, who have known him only in that room,
     are now amazed to see him in the bloom
of age, his paisley tie and gold stickpin

     flawlessly in place
as he picks up speed along the cinder runway,
     rises once more toward the bar, away
from rooms and lives he filled with ease and grace.

For Julia Randall

on her retirement from Hollins College, 1973

How Not To Domesticate Wildness might have been
the title for a course you never taught,
yet gave at every turn, with every breath
taking to heart the mind's life among ferns,
moles, birds, wild humans and Anglophile dogs.

I hear you say, *You make things with their names,*
but all these names are what get in the way.
What's the right word for how you leave us, then?
How shall I name a pleasurable regret?
I say the view changes, as you said it would.

Whenever I try to follow you out to the edges
of everything, hunting the words for praise,
I will find my way by stones that you have named.

Return to the Old Friends

This Meeting House, rising from a rejoicing
April landscape, is emptied of all music,
though sunlight glances brightly from the crimson
flowers by the road. We feel the hollow clash
of mystery in this liveliness, opposing
the final smallness of our hopes that peace

may be with him forever, whose life was peace.
My grandfather is here, beyond all the rejoicing
he carried into his legendary garden, opposing
the encroachment of things he had not planted, music
rising from around him in those days as the clash
of hoe on stone struck sparks of crimson

until the whole garden seemed stained crimson
with his foes' blood. Yet, by his labor, peace
flourished in his garden, until, as at a clash
of cymbals, we find him, far from all rejoicing;
we walk to our seats as to a solemn music.
Years have gone by since I left here, opposing

all that this house gave me while opposing
mysteries called me to other places, crimson
pageantries these Friends distrust. What music
did I look for when I left this house of peace,
shaking certain hands for the last time, rejoicing
in what I thought my victory in the old clash

with all that fathered me? I relive that clash,
trying to recall the force I was opposing
in my father's calm eyes as I fled rejoicing.

Now it is Easter, spring is green and crimson,
yet his father lies here. I come in peace
to greet old Friends once more, in search of music

that deserted me at my departure, music
free of pageantry or sound, without the clash
of bells that signal anything but peace.
My grandfather lies still as stone, opposing
my wish for breath below the touch of crimson,
yet in his presence now I stand rejoicing.

This silent music in my blood, opposing
the clash of sunlight dancing on crimson,
leads me toward peace and a strange rejoicing.

Bernard and Sarah

"Hang them where they'll do some good," my grandfather
said, as he placed the dusty photograph
in my father's hands. My father and I stared
at two old people posed stiffly side by side—
my great-great-great-grandparents, in the days
when photography was young, and they were not.
My father thought it out as we drove home.

Deciding that they might do the most good
somewhere out of sight, my father drove
a nail into the back wall of his closet;
they have hung there ever since, brought out
only on such occasions as the marriage
of one of his own children. "I think you ought
to know the stock you're joining with," he says.

Then back they go to the closet, where they hang
keeping their counsel until it is called for.
Yet, through walls, over miles of fields and woods
that flourish still around the farm they cleared,
their eyes light up the closet of my brain
to draw me toward the place I started from,
and when I have come home, they take me in.